How To Forgive

And Forget.

:

Cleanse Your Mind, Heal Your Heart, And Forget The Hurt To Embrace Inner Peace Of Mind And Move On.

My Message For You

To those who have been intentionally, irrationally, or inexplicably hurt by others, I extend my heartfelt empathy and understanding. It's often difficult to make sense of the pain inflicted upon us, especially when it seems unjust or unwarranted. Yet, in the face of such adversity, I urge you to remember your inherent worth and resilience.

Firstly, know that your pain is valid, and it's okay to acknowledge the hurt you've experienced. Allow yourself to feel and process your emotions without judgment or shame. Your feelings matter, and they deserve to be honored with compassion and kindness.

While it may seem tempting to hold onto resentment or seek revenge, I encourage you to consider the weight of carrying such burdens. Holding onto anger and bitterness only perpetuates the cycle of hurt and suffering. Instead, I invite you to explore the transformative power of forgiveness.

Forgiveness does not mean excusing or condoning the actions of those who have hurt you. Rather, it's a courageous act of liberation—a decision to reclaim your power and break free from the chains of resentment. By forgiving others, you release yourself from the grip of the past and open the door to healing and inner peace.

Moreover, remember that forgiveness is a journey, not a destination. It takes time, patience, and self-compassion to navigate the complexities of forgiveness. Be gentle with yourself as you embark on this path, and know that it's okay to seek support from trusted friends, family members, or professionals along the way.

As you embrace the journey of forgiveness, consider the profound impact it can have not only on your own well-being but also on the world around you. By choosing forgiveness, you become a beacon of hope and healing—a testament to the resilience of the human spirit.

Ultimately, your capacity to forgive is a testament to your strength and humanity. It's a powerful reminder that despite the pain we may endure, love and compassion have the power to transcend even the deepest wounds. May you find solace in the knowledge that healing is possible, and may you continue to journey toward a future filled with peace, joy, and wholeness.

Introduction

In the tapestry of human experience, woven with threads of joy, sorrow, love, and loss, forgiveness stands as a profound and transformative force—a beacon of hope amidst the shadows of pain and resentment. Welcome to "How **To Forgive And Forget: Cleanse Your Mind, Heal Your Heart, And Forget The Hurt To Embrace Inner Peace Of Mind And Move On."**

In the depths of our souls, we carry the weight of past grievances, wounds inflicted by others, and even the scars of our own missteps. These burdens, though invisible to the eye, can weigh heavy on our hearts, clouding our vision and hindering our ability to embrace the fullness of life.

But within the recesses of our being lies the profound potential for healing and renewal—a capacity to forgive and forget, not merely as acts of moral virtue, but as pathways to liberation and inner peace. This book is a guiding light for those who seek to embark on this sacred journey of forgiveness and forgetting.

Drawing upon wisdom from psychology, spirituality, and personal growth, "How To Forgive And Forget" offers practical insights, transformative exercises, and heartfelt guidance to help you navigate the complexities of forgiveness and release the grip of past hurts. It is a roadmap for cleansing your mind, healing your heart, and embracing the boundless possibilities that await on the other side of forgiveness.

Through the pages of this book, you will embark on a journey of self-discovery and healing—a journey that invites you to confront the shadows of resentment, to tenderly nurture the seeds of compassion, and to embrace the radiant light of forgiveness. You will explore the intricate tapestry of human emotions, unravel the knots of past grievances, and weave a new narrative of resilience, grace, and inner peace.

But forgiveness is not a destination—it is a dynamic and ongoing process that unfolds with each breath, each heartbeat, and each moment of presence. As you journey through these pages, may you find solace in the shared experiences of fellow travelers, inspiration in the wisdom of ancient teachings, and empowerment in the transformative power of forgiveness.

Together, let us embark on this sacred pilgrimage—a pilgrimage of forgiveness and forgetting—toward the shores of inner peace, where the waters of compassion flow freely, and the light of forgiveness illuminates the path to wholeness.

Table Of Contents

Chapter 1: The Liberation of Forgiveness

- Introduction to the transformative power of forgiveness.
- Exploring the mental and emotional burdens carried by unforgiveness.
- Understanding the difference between forgiveness and reconciliation.

Introduction to the transformative power of forgiveness.

In the human experience, forgiveness stands as a beacon of hope and resilience, offering the promise of liberation from the burdens of anger, resentment, and pain. It is a profound act of courage and compassion that has the power to transform hearts, mend relationships, and heal deep wounds. In this introduction, we embark on a journey to explore the transformative power of forgiveness—a journey that invites us to cleanse our minds, heal our hearts, and embrace inner peace.

The Weight of Unforgiveness: Unforgiveness weighs heavy on the soul, tethering us to the past and clouding our present with bitterness and sorrow. The wounds inflicted by betrayal, injustice, and hurtful actions can fester within us, eroding our sense of self-worth and diminishing our capacity for joy. As we carry the burden of unforgiveness, we find ourselves trapped in a cycle of resentment, unable to break free from the chains that bind us.

The Essence of Forgiveness: Forgiveness is a profound act of self-liberation—a choice to let go of the pain of the past and reclaim our power to shape our own destinies. It is not a condoning of wrongs or a denial of hurt; rather, it is a conscious decision to release ourselves from the grip of anger and resentment. In forgiving others, we honor our own humanity and affirm our inherent capacity for love and compassion.

The Healing Journey: Forgiveness is a journey—a process of healing and transformation that unfolds over time. It requires courage, vulnerability, and a willingness to confront the pain that lies buried within us. As we embark on this journey, we must be gentle with ourselves, recognizing that forgiveness is not always easy and that healing takes time. It is a journey of self-discovery and self-compassion—a journey that invites us to embrace our own humanity and extend grace to others.

The Power of Letting Go: Central to the process of forgiveness is the power of letting go—the willingness to release the grip of past hurts and embrace the possibility of a new beginning. Letting go doesn't mean forgetting or condoning; rather, it means freeing ourselves from the burden of carrying resentments and allowing ourselves to move forward with grace and dignity. In letting go, we create space for healing, growth, and renewal.

Embracing Inner Peace: At the heart of forgiveness lies the promise of inner peace—a deep sense of serenity and wholeness that transcends the pain of the past. As we cultivate forgiveness in our hearts, we open ourselves to the possibility of experiencing true joy, love, and connection. Inner peace is not the absence of conflict or pain; rather, it is the presence of acceptance, gratitude, and compassion—a sacred space where healing begins and transformation unfolds.

In the pages that follow, we will explore the multifaceted nature of forgiveness, delving into its profound impact on our lives and relationships. We will learn practical strategies for cultivating forgiveness, embracing inner peace, and moving forward with grace and resilience. Together, let us embark on this journey of healing and transformation—a journey guided by the transformative power of forgiveness.

Exploring the mental and emotional burdens carried by unforgiveness.

Unforgiveness is not merely the absence of forgiveness; it is an active state of holding onto grievances, resentments, and hurts from the past. It manifests as a heavy burden that weighs down the mind and heart, casting a shadow over our relationships, our well-being, and our overall quality of life. In this exploration, we delve into the intricate ways in which unforgiveness manifests its mental and emotional toll, shedding light on the profound impact it has on our inner landscape.

1. Chronic Stress and Anxiety: Unforgiveness is often accompanied by a constant state of stress and anxiety. The mind replays past hurts like a broken record, triggering a cascade of negative emotions and physiological responses. The body remains in a state of heightened alertness, perpetuating a cycle of tension and discomfort that takes a toll on our mental and physical health.

2. Resentment and Bitterness: At the core of unforgiveness lies resentment and bitterness—emotions that poison the soul and corrode our capacity for joy and compassion. Holding onto grudges keeps us tethered to the past, preventing us from fully engaging with the present moment and robbing us of the opportunity to experience genuine connection and intimacy with others.

3. Loss of Trust and Connection: Unforgiveness erodes trust and undermines the foundation of healthy relationships. When we harbor resentment towards others, we build walls of mistrust and suspicion, isolating ourselves from the possibility of authentic connection and intimacy. Our interactions become colored by past grievances, preventing us from truly opening our hearts to others and receiving the love and support we crave.

4. Negative Self-Image and Low Self-Esteem: The act of withholding forgiveness often reflects our own deep-seated insecurities and feelings of inadequacy. When we cannot forgive others, we may struggle to extend the same grace and compassion to ourselves, leading to feelings of self-doubt, unworthiness, and low self-esteem. Unforgiveness becomes a reflection of our own inner turmoil and self-imposed limitations.

5. Physical Symptoms and Health Complications: The toll of unforgiveness extends beyond the realm of the mind and emotions, manifesting in physical symptoms and health complications. Chronic stress, anxiety, and unresolved emotional trauma can contribute to a host of health issues, including hypertension, cardiovascular disease, and compromised immune function. The mind-body connection reminds us that our emotional well-being profoundly impacts our physical health.

In essence, unforgiveness exacts a steep price on our mental, emotional, and physical well-being, imprisoning us in a cycle of pain and suffering. It is only by acknowledging the profound impact of unforgiveness that we can begin to loosen its grip on our lives and embark on a journey of healing and liberation. In the chapters that follow, we will explore the transformative power of forgiveness—a journey that offers hope, healing, and the promise of a brighter tomorrow.

Understanding the difference between forgiveness and reconciliation.

Forgiveness and reconciliation are often used interchangeably, but they represent distinct concepts with unique implications for relationships and personal growth. In this exploration, we delve into the nuanced differences between forgiveness and reconciliation, shedding light on their respective meanings, purposes, and dynamics.

1. Forgiveness: Forgiveness is a deeply personal and internal process that involves letting go of resentment, anger, and bitterness towards someone who has wronged us. It is a conscious decision to release ourselves from the emotional burdens of the past and to cultivate compassion, empathy, and understanding towards the offender. Forgiveness does not necessarily require reconciliation or a restoration of trust; rather, it is a journey of healing and liberation that we embark on for our own well-being and peace of mind. By forgiving others, we reclaim our power to shape our own destinies and break free from the chains of unforgiveness.

2. Reconciliation: Reconciliation, on the other hand, is a relational process that involves the restoration of trust, harmony, and mutual respect between individuals or groups who have been estranged or in conflict. Unlike forgiveness, which is primarily focused on the inner state of the forgiver, reconciliation requires active engagement and communication between the parties involved. It entails a willingness to address past grievances, to seek understanding and empathy, and to work towards rebuilding a sense of connection and shared purpose. Reconciliation may involve apologies, restitution, and efforts to repair damaged relationships, but it is not always achievable or advisable in every situation.

<u>Key Differences:</u>

- Forgiveness is primarily an internal process, while reconciliation involves external actions and interactions between individuals or groups.

- Forgiveness is unconditional and can be granted even if the offender does not acknowledge wrongdoing or seek reconciliation.

- Reconciliation requires mutual consent and willingness from both parties to engage in dialogue, repair trust, and rebuild relationships.

- Forgiveness is often seen as a prerequisite for reconciliation, but it is possible to forgive without reconciling with the offender, especially in cases where reconciliation may not be safe or feasible.

The Interplay Between Forgiveness and Reconciliation: While forgiveness and reconciliation are distinct concepts, they are often interconnected and can influence each other in complex ways. Forgiveness may pave the way for reconciliation by creating a foundation of trust and empathy, but reconciliation is not always necessary for forgiveness to occur. Conversely, reconciliation may facilitate deeper levels of forgiveness by providing opportunities for healing, understanding, and mutual growth.

In summary, forgiveness and reconciliation represent complementary paths towards healing, restoration, and peace. By understanding the nuances of each concept, we empower ourselves to navigate the complexities of relationships with wisdom, compassion, and integrity, embracing forgiveness as a journey of self-discovery and reconciliation as a process of healing and renewal.

Chapter 2: Acknowledging the Pain

- **Delving into the importance of acknowledging and validating your own pain.**
- **Recognizing the impact of the hurt on your well-being.**
- **How facing the pain is the first step towards genuine forgiveness.**

Delving into the importance of acknowledging and validating your own pain.

In the intricate landscape of emotional healing, the journey begins with the courageous act of acknowledging and validating your own pain. This process is not merely a superficial recognition of discomfort; rather, it is a profound and transformative journey of self-discovery and self-compassion. In this exploration, we delve into the importance of acknowledging and validating your own pain as a crucial step towards healing and personal growth.

1. Honoring Your Truth: Acknowledging and validating your own pain is an act of honoring your truth—the reality of your experiences, emotions, and struggles. It is an affirmation of your inherent worth and dignity as a human being, deserving of compassion, empathy, and understanding. By acknowledging your pain, you reclaim your voice and agency, refusing to be silenced or invalidated by external forces or societal expectations.

2. Embracing Vulnerability: Acknowledging and validating your own pain requires a willingness to embrace vulnerability—the courage to confront the raw and unfiltered emotions that lie beneath the surface. It is an invitation to lean into discomfort, uncertainty, and discomfort, recognizing that vulnerability is not a sign of weakness but a catalyst for growth and transformation. By embracing vulnerability, you create space for authenticity, connection, and genuine self-expression.

3. Cultivating Self-Compassion: Self-compassion lies at the heart of acknowledging and validating your own pain. It is the gentle and loving response to your own suffering—the recognition that you are worthy of kindness, acceptance, and care, especially in times of difficulty and distress. By cultivating self-compassion, you nurture resilience, self-awareness, and emotional well-being, fostering a deep sense of inner peace and wholeness.

4. Breaking the Cycle of Denial and Suppression: Denying or suppressing your pain only perpetuates the cycle of suffering and stagnation. Unacknowledged pain festers beneath the surface, manifesting in various forms of physical and emotional distress, including anxiety, depression, and chronic stress. By courageously acknowledging and validating your own pain, you break free from the grip of denial and suppression, reclaiming your power to heal and transform your life.

5. Fostering Authentic Connection: Authentic connection with others begins with a deep and genuine connection with yourself. By acknowledging and validating your own pain, you cultivate authenticity, vulnerability, and empathy—the foundations of meaningful relationships and genuine human connection. Your willingness to share your struggles and vulnerabilities creates a safe space for others to do the same, fostering a sense of belonging and mutual support.

In essence, acknowledging and validating your own pain is an essential step on the path to healing, self-discovery, and personal empowerment. It is a journey of courage, compassion, and self-acceptance—a journey that invites you to embrace the fullness of your humanity and to reclaim your inherent resilience and strength. By honoring your truth and embracing your vulnerabilities, you pave the way for profound transformation and the emergence of a life filled with authenticity, purpose, and inner peace.

<u>Recognizing the impact of the hurt on your well-being.</u>

Hurt, whether inflicted by others or arising from life's inevitable challenges, can have profound effects on our mental, emotional, and physical well-being. Recognizing the impact of hurt on your overall health and quality of life is a crucial step toward healing and restoration. In this exploration, we delve into the multifaceted ways in which hurt can influence your well-being and the importance of acknowledging its effects.

1. Emotional Distress: Hurt often triggers a range of intense emotions, including sadness, anger, fear, and despair. These emotions can become overwhelming, leading to emotional distress and turmoil. Persistent hurt may contribute to symptoms of depression, anxiety, and other mood disorders, affecting your ability to experience joy, peace, and fulfillment in life.

2. Disrupted Relationships: Hurt can strain relationships with family members, friends, romantic partners, and colleagues. When left unresolved, hurt may lead to resentment, mistrust, and communication breakdowns, eroding the foundation of healthy connections. Disrupted relationships can further exacerbate feelings of isolation, loneliness, and disconnection, impacting your sense of belonging and social support.

3. Physical Health Consequences: The effects of hurt extend beyond the realm of emotions and relationships, manifesting in physical health consequences. Chronic stress, triggered by unresolved hurt, can weaken the immune system, increase inflammation, and contribute to a host of health conditions, including cardiovascular disease, gastrointestinal disorders, and chronic pain. Addressing emotional pain is essential for promoting overall physical well-being.

4. Cognitive Distortions: Hurt can distort your perceptions of yourself, others, and the world around you. Negative beliefs about trust, worthiness, and safety may emerge, influencing your thoughts and behaviors in various aspects of life. Cognitive distortions perpetuate patterns of negative thinking, self-criticism, and self-doubt, hindering your ability to experience self-compassion, resilience, and personal growth.

5. Impaired Coping Mechanisms: In response to hurt, individuals may develop maladaptive coping mechanisms, such as substance abuse, avoidance behaviors, or self-harm. These coping strategies provide temporary relief but ultimately perpetuate cycles of suffering and dysfunction. Recognizing the impact of hurt on your coping mechanisms empowers you to seek healthier alternatives, such as therapy, mindfulness practices, and social support networks.

6. Diminished Self-Concept: Hurt can erode your sense of self-worth, identity, and purpose. Negative experiences may fuel feelings of shame, guilt, and inadequacy, distorting your perception of your own value and potential. Reclaiming a positive self-concept requires acknowledging the impact of hurt and cultivating self-compassion, self-awareness, and self-acceptance.

In essence, recognizing the impact of hurt on your well-being is the first step toward initiating the healing process. By acknowledging the emotional, relational, physical, cognitive, and behavioral consequences of hurt, you validate your own experiences and affirm your inherent worthiness of healing and restoration. Through self-reflection, self-care, and seeking support from trusted individuals or professionals, you can embark on a journey of healing, resilience, and growth, reclaiming your capacity to thrive and flourish in the face of adversity.

How facing the pain is the first step towards genuine forgiveness.

Facing the pain is indeed the crucial first step towards genuine forgiveness. When we confront the pain caused by past hurts and wounds, we acknowledge the depth of our emotional suffering and begin the process of healing. Here's why facing the pain is essential on the path to forgiveness:

1. Acknowledgment of Reality: Facing the pain involves acknowledging the reality of what happened and its impact on our lives. It's about being honest with ourselves about the hurt we've experienced and not minimizing or denying its significance. By facing the pain, we confront the truth of our emotional wounds and the ways in which they have affected us.

2. Validation of Feelings: Confronting the pain validates our feelings and experiences. It allows us to honor the validity of our emotions, whether they be anger, sadness, betrayal, or resentment. Validating our feelings doesn't mean we have to justify them; rather, it's about giving ourselves permission to feel and express our emotions authentically.

3. Release of Emotional Energy: Unaddressed pain can become like a heavy weight that we carry with us everywhere we go. By facing the pain, we begin to release the pent-up emotional energy that has been holding us back. Expressing our emotions, whether through journaling, therapy, or conversations with trusted individuals, allows us to let go of what no longer serves us.

4. Understanding the Root Cause: Facing the pain enables us to understand the root cause of our suffering. We can explore the underlying beliefs, traumas, and patterns that have contributed to our emotional wounds. Understanding the root cause helps us make sense of our experiences and empowers us to address them from a place of compassion and self-awareness.

5. Empowerment to Choose Forgiveness: When we face the pain, we reclaim our power to choose how we respond to it. Rather than allowing the pain to dictate our actions and attitudes, we become active participants in our healing journey. Confronting the pain opens the door to forgiveness by creating space for compassion, empathy, and understanding to flourish.

6. Transformation and Healing: Ultimately, facing the pain is a transformative process that leads to healing and growth. It requires courage and vulnerability to confront the aspects of ourselves that we'd rather avoid. Yet, it is through this process that we can release the grip of the past and embrace a future filled with possibility, freedom, and inner peace.

In summary, facing the pain is not easy, but it is a necessary step on the path to genuine forgiveness. It requires courage, self-compassion, and a willingness to confront our deepest emotions. By acknowledging the pain, we create the foundation for forgiveness to take root and flourish, paving the way for profound healing and liberation of the heart.

Chapter 3: The Anatomy of Forgiveness

- **Breaking down the components of forgiveness.**
- **The role of empathy and understanding in the forgiveness process.**
- **Building compassion for yourself and others.**

Breaking down the components of forgiveness.

Breaking down the components of forgiveness reveals its multifaceted nature, encompassing cognitive, emotional, and behavioral elements. Here are the key components:

Acknowledgment of Hurt: The first component involves recognizing and acknowledging the hurt or harm caused by the offender. This acknowledgment validates the pain experienced and serves as a starting point for the forgiveness process.

Acceptance of Emotions: Forgiveness involves accepting and allowing oneself to experience a range of emotions associated with the hurt, including anger, sadness, and betrayal. Rather than suppressing or denying these emotions, forgiveness entails acknowledging and processing them in a healthy manner.

Empathy and Compassion: Central to forgiveness is the cultivation of empathy and compassion toward the offender. It involves trying to understand the perspective of the person who caused the harm, recognizing their humanity, and acknowledging that they, too, may be struggling or imperfect.

Letting Go of Resentment: Forgiveness requires a conscious decision to let go of resentment and bitterness towards the offender. It involves releasing the desire for revenge or retribution and relinquishing the power that the hurt holds over one's thoughts and emotions.

Choosing to Forgive: Forgiveness is ultimately a choice—a deliberate decision to extend grace and mercy to the offender despite the pain they have caused. It involves recognizing one's own agency and autonomy in deciding to release the burden of unforgiveness.

Setting Boundaries: Forgiveness does not necessarily mean condoning or excusing the harmful behavior of the offender. It may involve setting healthy boundaries to protect oneself from further harm and establishing expectations for future interactions.

Seeking Meaning and Growth: Forgiveness can be a transformative process that fosters personal growth and resilience. It may involve finding meaning and lessons in the experience of hurt, identifying areas for self-improvement, and using the pain as a catalyst for positive change.

Reconciliation (Optional): While forgiveness and reconciliation are related, they are distinct concepts. Reconciliation involves restoring trust and repairing the relationship with the offender, which may or may not be possible or advisable depending on the circumstances.

Release of Grudges: Forgiveness entails releasing grudges and resentments that can poison relationships and hinder personal well-being. It involves freeing oneself from the burden of carrying past grievances and embracing a future unencumbered by bitterness.

In summary, forgiveness is a complex and multifaceted process that involves acknowledging hurt, accepting emotions, cultivating empathy and compassion, letting go of resentment, making a conscious choice to forgive, setting boundaries, seeking growth, and optionally, pursuing reconciliation. By understanding these components, individuals can embark on a journey of healing, liberation, and inner peace.

The role of empathy and understanding in the forgiveness process.

Empathy and understanding play pivotal roles in the forgiveness process, facilitating healing, reconciliation, and emotional well-being. Here's how empathy and understanding contribute to forgiveness:

Promoting Perspective-Taking: Empathy allows individuals to step into the shoes of the offender and see the situation from their perspective. By understanding the motivations, emotions, and circumstances that may have led to the hurtful behavior, individuals can develop a more nuanced understanding of the situation and the factors at play.

Humanizing the Offender: Empathy humanizes the offender, recognizing their inherent humanity and capacity for both kindness and mistakes. It acknowledges that everyone is fallible and capable of making errors in judgment or causing harm unintentionally. Seeing the offender as a complex individual rather than solely as a perpetrator of harm can foster compassion and forgiveness.

Facilitating Emotional Connection: Empathy creates an emotional connection between the victim and the offender, fostering a sense of shared humanity and interconnectedness. Recognizing the commonality of human experiences—such as pain, fear, and vulnerability—can dissolve barriers and animosities, paving the way for empathy-based forgiveness.

Fostering Compassion: Understanding the circumstances and emotions surrounding the hurtful act can evoke feelings of compassion and empathy toward the offender. Rather than responding with anger or retaliation, individuals may choose to extend kindness, mercy, and understanding, recognizing the potential for growth and redemption.

Breaking the Cycle of Resentment: Empathy disrupts the cycle of resentment and bitterness by providing a pathway to understanding and reconciliation. It allows individuals to release the grip of anger and hostility, replacing negative emotions with empathy, compassion, and forgiveness.

Promoting Healing and Closure: Empathetic forgiveness promotes healing and closure for both the victim and the offender. It acknowledges the pain caused by the hurtful act while also recognizing the potential for healing and reconciliation. By fostering understanding and empathy, individuals can find peace and resolution, freeing themselves from the burden of unforgiveness.

Building Trust and Repairing Relationships: Understanding the perspective of the offender and empathizing with their experiences can lay the foundation for rebuilding trust and repairing damaged relationships. Empathetic forgiveness opens the door to honest communication, vulnerability, and mutual understanding, fostering stronger and more resilient connections.

In summary, empathy and understanding are essential components of the forgiveness process, promoting healing, reconciliation, and emotional well-being. By cultivating empathy toward both oneself and others, individuals can transcend the cycle of hurt and resentment, fostering compassion, connection, and forgiveness in their relationships and communities.

Building compassion for yourself and others.

Building compassion for yourself and others is a fundamental aspect of the forgiveness process and is essential for fostering healing, understanding, and connection. Here's how you can cultivate compassion in your life:

Practice Self-Compassion: Start by extending kindness, understanding, and support to yourself, especially during times of struggle or difficulty. Treat yourself with the same level of compassion and empathy that you would offer to a friend facing similar challenges. Practice self-care activities that nurture your physical, emotional, and spiritual well-being.

Cultivate Mindfulness: Mindfulness involves being present and aware of your thoughts, emotions, and experiences without judgment. By cultivating mindfulness through practices such as meditation, yoga, or deep breathing exercises, you can develop greater awareness of your inner experiences and respond to yourself and others with compassion and acceptance.

Challenge Negative Self-Talk: Pay attention to your internal dialogue and challenge negative self-talk or self-criticism. Replace harsh judgments with words of encouragement, affirmation, and self-compassion. Recognize that imperfection is part of the human experience and that mistakes are opportunities for growth and learning.

Practice Forgiveness: Forgiveness is an act of compassion—toward both yourself and others. Release yourself from the burden of holding onto grudges and resentments by practicing forgiveness. Recognize that forgiveness is a gift you give to yourself, allowing you to let go of the past and embrace the present with openness and acceptance.

Seek Common Humanity: Recognize the shared humanity that connects us all. Understand that everyone experiences pain, suffering, and vulnerability at some point in their lives. By acknowledging our common humanity, you can cultivate empathy and compassion toward others, even in challenging situations.

Practice Empathetic Listening: Listen to others with empathy and an open heart. Seek to understand their perspectives, emotions, and experiences without judgment or interruption. Validate their feelings and offer support and encouragement when needed. Empathetic listening strengthens connections and fosters trust and understanding in relationships.

Acts of Kindness and Generosity: Engage in acts of kindness and generosity toward yourself and others. Small gestures of compassion, such as offering a listening ear, expressing gratitude, or performing random acts of kindness, can have a profound impact on your well-being and the well-being of those around you.

Set Boundaries with Compassion: Establish healthy boundaries in your relationships with compassion and respect. Communicate your needs, preferences, and limits assertively and empathetically. Setting boundaries is an act of self-care that honors your well-being while also respecting the autonomy and boundaries of others.

In summary, building compassion for yourself and others is a transformative practice that promotes healing, understanding, and connection. By cultivating compassion in your life, you create a nurturing environment where forgiveness, empathy, and acceptance can flourish, fostering greater peace, resilience, and fulfillment.

Chapter 4: The Elusive Art of Forgetting

- The challenge of forgetting and why it's crucial for true healing.
- Understanding how memories contribute to emotional wounds.
- Exploring methods to gradually release the grip of painful memories.

<u>The challenge of forgetting and why it's crucial for true healing.</u>

The challenge of forgetting is indeed a significant hurdle on the path to true healing, especially in the context of forgiveness and overcoming past hurts. While forgetting may seem elusive or even impossible, it plays a crucial role in the process of healing and moving forward. Here's why forgetting is essential for genuine healing:

Release from Emotional Bondage: Memories of past hurts can keep us emotionally tethered to the pain of the past, preventing us from fully embracing the present and future. The challenge of forgetting lies in freeing ourselves from the emotional bondage of past traumas, allowing us to experience emotional liberation and inner peace.

Prevention of Ruminative Patterns: Dwelling on past hurts and grievances can perpetuate rumination—a pattern of repetitive, negative thoughts and emotions that can undermine mental and emotional well-being. The challenge of forgetting involves breaking free from rumination and cultivating a mindset focused on growth, resilience, and positive change.

Creation of Mental Space for Healing:
Holding onto painful memories occupies
mental space and energy that could
otherwise be devoted to healing, growth,
and self-discovery. The challenge of
forgetting is about creating room in our
minds and hearts for new experiences,
perspectives, and possibilities, allowing us
to embrace life with renewed vitality and
purpose.

Restoration of Trust and Vulnerability:
Lingering memories of past hurts can erode
trust and intimacy in relationships, making it
difficult to be vulnerable and open to
connection. The challenge of forgetting
involves letting go of past grievances and
allowing ourselves to trust again—to trust in
the inherent goodness of others and in our
own capacity for resilience and growth.

Promotion of Emotional Resilience:
Dwelling on past hurts can weaken our
emotional resilience and adaptive coping

mechanisms, making us more susceptible to stress, anxiety, and depression. The challenge of forgetting requires us to cultivate emotional resilience by letting go of resentments and embracing a mindset of forgiveness, acceptance, and gratitude.

Embrace of the Present Moment: The challenge of forgetting is ultimately about embracing the present moment fully and wholeheartedly. It involves letting go of regrets about the past and anxieties about the future, and instead, savoring the beauty, joy, and opportunities that exist in the here and now.

Freedom to Create a New Narrative: Forgetting empowers us to create a new narrative for our lives—one that is rooted in forgiveness, compassion, and self-love. It allows us to rewrite the story of our past from a place of strength and resilience, rather than being defined by our wounds and traumas.

In summary, the challenge of forgetting is an integral part of the healing journey—a journey that invites us to release the grip of the past and embrace the possibility of a brighter, more fulfilling future. While forgetting may be difficult, it is also essential for true healing, resilience, and the restoration of hope and wholeness in our lives.

Understanding how memories contribute to emotional wounds.

Memories play a profound role in shaping our emotional experiences and can contribute significantly to emotional wounds. Here's how memories contribute to the formation and persistence of emotional wounds:

Encoding of Emotional Events: Memories are formed through the encoding of emotional events in the brain. When we experience significant or traumatic events, our brains encode the associated emotions, sensations, and perceptions into memory. These emotional memories can be vivid and intense, influencing our thoughts, feelings, and behaviors long after the initial event has occurred.

Association with Triggers: Emotional wounds often become linked to specific triggers—people, places, smells, sounds, or situations that evoke memories of the original traumatic event. These triggers can reignite the emotional pain associated with the past, causing distress and discomfort in the present moment. The association between memories and triggers reinforces the emotional intensity of the wounds.

Intrusive Thoughts and Flashbacks: Memories of traumatic events can manifest as intrusive thoughts, flashbacks, or nightmares, intruding into our consciousness and reawakening painful emotions. These intrusive memories can be distressing and overwhelming, disrupting our ability to function effectively in daily life and exacerbating feelings of anxiety, depression, or post-traumatic stress.

Negative Interpretation and Rumination: Emotional wounds often lead to negative interpretations of oneself, others, and the world. Memories of past hurts can fuel rumination—a pattern of repetitive, negative thoughts and interpretations that reinforce feelings of helplessness, hopelessness, and worthlessness. Rumination perpetuates the cycle of emotional wounds, amplifying their impact on our mental and emotional well-being.

Impact on Relationships: Memories of past hurts can influence our perceptions and interactions in current relationships. We may project past relational patterns onto new relationships, leading to mistrust, fear of intimacy, or difficulty in forming meaningful connections. The emotional baggage carried from past wounds can strain relationships and hinder emotional intimacy and vulnerability.

Cognitive Biases and Distortions: Memories of emotional wounds are susceptible to cognitive biases and distortions that shape our perceptions of reality. Confirmation bias, for example, may lead us to selectively attend to information that confirms our negative beliefs about ourselves or others, reinforcing the emotional wounds we carry. These cognitive biases distort our interpretation of events and perpetuate negative thought patterns.

Difficulty in Letting Go: Emotional wounds can become deeply ingrained in our sense of identity and self-concept, making it challenging to let go of the associated memories and emotions. The fear of vulnerability, rejection, or further hurt may lead us to cling to the familiar discomfort of our emotional wounds, even when they no longer serve us.

In summary, memories contribute to emotional wounds by encoding traumatic events, associating with triggers, manifesting as intrusive thoughts and flashbacks, fueling negative interpretation and rumination, influencing relationships, perpetuating cognitive biases and distortions, and creating difficulty in letting go. Recognizing the role of memories in the formation and persistence of emotional wounds is essential for understanding their impact and initiating the healing process.

Exploring methods to gradually release the grip of painful memories.

Releasing the grip of painful memories is a gradual and transformative process that involves self-awareness, self-compassion, and intentional healing practices. Here are several methods to explore in order to gradually release the hold of painful memories:

Mindfulness Meditation: Mindfulness meditation cultivates present-moment awareness and acceptance of thoughts, emotions, and sensations without judgment. By observing painful memories with compassion and detachment, you can gradually diminish their emotional charge and create space for healing and inner peace.

Cognitive Behavioral Therapy (CBT): CBT techniques help challenge and reframe negative thought patterns associated with painful memories. Through cognitive restructuring and behavioral interventions, you can develop healthier coping strategies and reduce the emotional intensity of distressing memories over time.

Emotional Processing Techniques: Engage in emotional processing techniques such as journaling, expressive writing, or creative arts therapy to explore and process painful memories in a safe and supportive environment. Expressing your emotions through writing, drawing, or other forms of creative expression can facilitate catharsis and release.

Forgiveness Practice: Practice forgiveness as a way to release the grip of painful memories and cultivate compassion for yourself and others. By acknowledging the humanity of those who have caused harm and letting go of resentment and bitterness, you can free yourself from the emotional burden of past grievances.

Grounding Exercises: Grounding techniques help anchor you in the present moment and reduce the intensity of distressing memories. Use sensory-based grounding exercises such as deep breathing, progressive muscle relaxation, or visualization to shift your focus away from painful memories and connect with your immediate surroundings.

Self-Compassion Practices: Cultivate self-compassion by offering kindness, understanding, and support to yourself as you navigate painful memories. Treat yourself with the same level of compassion and care that you would offer to a dear friend facing similar challenges. Practice self-soothing techniques and affirmations to nurture your inner resilience and well-being.

Seeking Professional Support: Consider seeking support from a therapist, counselor, or support group specializing in trauma and healing. Professional guidance can provide you with personalized strategies, validation, and encouragement as you work through painful memories and develop resilience.

Creating New Positive Memories: Intentionally engage in activities and experiences that create new positive memories and associations. Surround yourself with supportive relationships, engage in hobbies and interests that bring you joy, and explore new opportunities for growth and connection. Building a reservoir of positive experiences can counterbalance the weight of painful memories and promote emotional healing.

Practicing Acceptance and Letting Go: Practice acceptance of painful memories as part of your personal history without allowing them to define your present or future. Embrace the process of letting go—a gradual release of attachment to the past and an openness to new possibilities for growth, healing, and transformation.

In summary, releasing the grip of painful memories is a journey of self-discovery, resilience, and healing. By incorporating mindfulness, therapy, emotional processing techniques, forgiveness practices, grounding exercises, self-compassion, professional support, creating new positive memories, and practicing acceptance and letting go, you can gradually release the hold of painful memories and reclaim your capacity for joy, peace, and wholeness.

Chapter 5: Mindfulness and Present Moment Living

- **Introducing mindfulness as a powerful tool for letting go of the past.**
- **Techniques for staying present and cultivating a mind free from lingering resentment.**
- **The connection between mindfulness and the forgetting aspect of forgiveness.**

Introducing mindfulness as a powerful tool for letting go of the past.

Introducing mindfulness as a powerful tool for letting go of the past can open up new pathways to healing, resilience, and inner peace. Mindfulness involves cultivating present-moment awareness and acceptance of our thoughts, emotions, and experiences without judgment. Here's how mindfulness can facilitate the process of letting go of the past:

Awareness of Thought Patterns: Mindfulness helps us become aware of the repetitive thought patterns and rumination associated with past experiences. By observing our thoughts with curiosity and non-judgment, we can begin to recognize how clinging to the past keeps us stuck in cycles of suffering.

Acceptance of Emotions: Mindfulness encourages us to acknowledge and accept the full range of emotions that arise when reflecting on the past. Rather than suppressing or avoiding difficult emotions, we learn to embrace them with compassion and understanding, allowing them to come and go without resistance.

Non-Identification with Thoughts and Feelings: Through mindfulness, we develop the ability to observe our thoughts and feelings as passing phenomena rather than absolute truths. We come to understand that we are not defined by our past experiences or the stories we tell ourselves about them.

Cultivation of Equanimity: Mindfulness fosters a sense of equanimity—the ability to remain balanced and centered in the face of life's ups and downs. As we practice mindfulness, we learn to respond to challenging memories and emotions with greater calmness, resilience, and clarity.

Living in the Present Moment: Mindfulness anchors us in the present moment, freeing us from the grip of past regrets and future anxieties. By focusing our attention on the here and now, we let go of attachments to the past and open ourselves to the richness of present-moment experiences.

Appreciation of Impermanence: Mindfulness teaches us to recognize the impermanent nature of all phenomena, including our thoughts, emotions, and memories. We come to understand that nothing remains static or unchanged, and that even the most painful memories will eventually fade with time.

Embracing Self-Compassion: Mindfulness encourages self-compassion—the practice of treating ourselves with kindness, warmth, and understanding, especially in moments of struggle or pain. By extending compassion to ourselves, we create a supportive inner environment for the process of letting go to unfold.

Freedom from Attachment: Mindfulness invites us to release attachments to the past—the stories, identities, and beliefs that no longer serve our growth and well-being. Through mindful awareness, we cultivate a sense of spaciousness and freedom, allowing us to let go of what no longer aligns with our present truth.

In summary, mindfulness offers a transformative path for letting go of the past and embracing the fullness of the present moment. By cultivating present-moment awareness, acceptance, equanimity, and self-compassion, we create the inner conditions for healing, resilience, and authentic living. Mindfulness empowers us to release the grip of the past and step into a future filled with possibility, growth, and profound inner peace.

<u>Techniques for staying present and cultivating a mind free from lingering resentment.</u>

It takes a mix of self-awareness, purposeful practices that promote acceptance and compassion, and mindfulness skills to stay present and cultivate a mind free from residual bitterness. Here are a few methods to assist you in letting go of grudges and being in the moment:

Mindful Breathing: Engage in mindful breathing techniques as a way to ground oneself in the here and now. Allow each inhale and exhalation to help you stay grounded in the present moment as you pay attention to the feelings of your breath as it enters and exits your body. To help you relax and center yourself, bring your focus back to your breathing whenever you sense resentment starting to surface.

Body Scan Meditation: To increase your awareness of your body's physical sensations, practice body scan meditations. Beginning at the top of your head, work your way down, paying attention to any spots that seem tight or uncomfortable. You may alleviate physical stress and enhance your experience with more presence and relaxation by learning to listen to your body's messages.

Observing ideas Judgment-Free: Work on observing your ideas free from attachment or bias. When bitter ideas come to mind, recognize them without allowing their meaning to consume you. Remember that thoughts are fleeting mental occurrences and that you are in control of how you react to them. Develop an open mind and a curious approach regarding your inner experiences.

Thankfulness Practice: To change your perspective from resentment to appreciation, establish a regular practice of thankfulness. Every day, set aside some time to consider the things for which you are thankful, no matter how little or unimportant they may appear. You may develop an attitude of plenty and happiness by focusing on the benefits and good things in your life.

Self-Compassion activities: To develop kindness and understanding toward oneself, engage in self-compassion activities. Give yourself the same consideration and understanding that you would give a friend going through a comparable situation. When emotions of resentment surface, use self-soothing methods like putting your palm over your heart or telling yourself encouraging words.

Forgiveness Meditation: Practice forgiveness meditation to develop compassion and let go of grudges toward others and yourself. Imagine the person or circumstance that has hurt you, then extend forgiveness to them from a place of sincere understanding and compassion. As you offer forgiveness, say something like, "May you find peace and be free from suffering."

Setting limits: To keep yourself safe from more injury and to stop resentment from ever starting in the first place, set up appropriate limits. When necessary, assertively stand up for yourself and let people know what you need and what your boundaries are. Establishing boundaries gives you the ability to put your health first and keep up positive connections.

Seeking Support: When navigating emotions of resentment, reach out to dependable friends, family members, or mental health experts for advice and support. Openly and honestly discuss your experiences with those who can relate, validate, and provide insight. Keep in mind that you don't have to handle challenging feelings by yourself.

You may develop a mind free of lingering resentment and adopt a present-centered lifestyle with more serenity, clarity, and compassion by incorporating these practices into your everyday life. It's important to keep in mind that getting over a grudge is a long process that calls for perseverance, introspection, and a dedication to your own mental health.

The connection between mindfulness and the forgetting aspect of forgiveness.

The connection between mindfulness and the forgetting aspect of forgiveness lies in the cultivation of present-moment awareness and the intentional release of attachment to past grievances. Mindfulness practices help individuals develop the capacity to observe their thoughts, emotions, and experiences without judgment, allowing them to let go of the stories and narratives that keep them tethered to the past. Here's how mindfulness contributes to the forgetting aspect of forgiveness:

Awareness of Thought Patterns: Mindfulness enables individuals to become aware of repetitive thought patterns associated with past hurts and grievances. By observing these patterns with curiosity and non-judgment, individuals can recognize how dwelling on the past perpetuates suffering and impedes their ability to experience peace in the present moment.

Acceptance of Emotions: Mindfulness encourages individuals to acknowledge and accept the full range of emotions that arise when reflecting on past experiences. Rather than suppressing or denying these emotions, individuals learn to hold them with compassion and understanding, allowing them to naturally arise and pass away without clinging to them.

Non-Identification with Thoughts and Feelings: Through mindfulness, individuals develop the ability to observe their thoughts and feelings as transient mental events rather than absolute truths. By recognizing that they are not defined by their past experiences or the stories they tell themselves about them, individuals can release identification with painful memories and create space for healing and growth.

Living in the Present Moment: Mindfulness anchors individuals in the present moment, freeing them from the grip of past regrets and future anxieties. By directing their attention to the here and now, individuals let go of attachments to the past and open themselves to the richness of present-moment experiences, fostering a sense of spaciousness and freedom.

Appreciation of Impermanence: Mindfulness teaches individuals to recognize the impermanent nature of all phenomena, including thoughts, emotions, and memories. By understanding that nothing remains static or unchanged, individuals come to see that even the most painful memories will eventually fade with time, allowing them to let go and move forward with greater ease.

Embracing Self-Compassion: Mindfulness invites individuals to extend compassion to themselves as they navigate the process of forgiveness. By treating themselves with kindness, warmth, and understanding, individuals create a supportive inner environment for releasing attachment to the past and embracing the possibilities of the present moment.

In summary, mindfulness serves as a powerful tool for fostering the forgetting aspect of forgiveness by cultivating present-moment awareness, acceptance of emotions, non-identification with thoughts and feelings, living in the present moment, appreciation of impermanence, and embracing self-compassion. Through mindfulness practices, individuals can release the grip of past grievances and open themselves to the transformative power of forgiveness, fostering greater peace, resilience, and well-being in their lives.

Chapter 6: Rewriting Your Narrative

- **Examining the stories we tell ourselves about the past.**
- **How reframing your narrative contributes to the process of forgetting.**
- **Cultivating a positive and empowering perspective on past experiences.**

Examining the stories we tell ourselves about the past.

One of the most important steps in developing self-awareness, healing, and personal development is to examine the narratives we tell ourselves about our history. Our current views, feelings, and actions are shaped by the narratives and interpretations we have about historical events. Examining these tales is crucial for the following reasons:

Recognizing Our Perspectives: Our own viewpoints, convictions, and life experiences often influence the narratives we tell ourselves about the past. We may learn more about how our own prejudices, presumptions, and prior conditioning may affect how we see and understand the world by looking at these tales.

Finding Recurring Patterns and Themes: By analyzing our stories, we may spot themes and patterns that may be present in our daily lives. These patterns might provide hints about repressed emotions, unfulfilled wants, and underlying concerns that may be affecting our actions and thoughts right now.

Examining Emotional Triggers: The tales we tell about our history may act as emotional triggers, bringing up intense emotions such as guilt, shame, rage, or despair. We may identify the underlying reasons for our discomfort and start addressing them with compassion and understanding by looking into the stories that underlie these emotional responses.

Taking On Limiting Beliefs: Negative self-perceptions or limiting beliefs may sometimes serve as the foundation for the tales we tell ourselves about the past. By shedding light on these ideas and investigating their roots, we may question their veracity and investigate other viewpoints that encourage personal development and empowerment.

Promoting Forgiveness and Healing: By analyzing our experiences, we may investigate the effects of previous setbacks, wounds, and disappointments on our present and future selves. By this process, we may let go of any emotional weights that could be dragging us down and develop empathy, compassion, and forgiveness—for both ourselves and others.

Developing New Narratives: By critically analyzing our experiences, we may establish new narratives that more closely reflect our beliefs, objectives, and ambitions. By rewriting the narratives of our history from a position of strength, resiliency, and authenticity, we may give ourselves the ability to live more purposefully and mindfully in the now and now.

Improving Self-Awareness: In the end, investigating the narratives we tell ourselves about the past helps us become more self-aware and cultivates a stronger feeling of inner knowledge and clarity. It opens the door for personal development and change by inviting us to investigate the intricacies of the human experience with openness and curiosity.

To sum up, looking into the stories we tell ourselves about the past can help us become more aware of our viewpoints, identify patterns and themes, investigate emotional triggers, confront limiting beliefs, promote forgiveness and healing, develop new narratives, and become more self-aware. Through courageous and compassionate participation in this process, we may foster increased resilience, authenticity, and overall well-being in our lives.

How reframing your narrative contributes to the process of forgetting.

By altering your perception of the past, letting go of unpleasant memories, and promoting a feeling of freedom and inner peace, reframing your story may greatly aid in the process of forgetting. Here's how rewriting your story speeds up the forgetting process:

Creating Distance from the Past: By reinterpreting your story, you may put the past behind you and see it from a different angle. You may reframe prior events such that they highlight learning, development, and resilience instead of defining or limiting you. This change in viewpoint promotes a forward-thinking attitude and helps release the hold that sad memories have on one.

Modifying the Emotional Charge: You may modify the emotional charge attached to previous occurrences by rewriting your story. You may practice cultivating sentiments of compassion, forgiveness, and acceptance rather than lingering on thoughts of resentment, regret, or fury. The intensity of painful memories is lessened by this emotional shift, which also makes it easier to let go and go on.

Finding the Silver Linings and Lessons: By rewriting your story, you may find the lessons and silver linings that are concealed inside difficult situations. You may derive meaning and purpose from previous hardships by acknowledging the chances for development and insight that come from adversity. This optimistic reading reframes failures as stepping stones toward resilience and personal growth.

Empowering Self-Identity: By rewriting your story, you give yourself the ability to reinterpret who you are in light of your history. You may take back control of your life narrative and recover agency from the idea that you are a victim of your circumstances. By emphasizing your abilities, fortitude, and potential for development, you build self-confidence and future-focused optimism.

Promoting Cognitive Flexibility: Reframing your story may help you become more cognitively flexible, which is the capacity to modify your viewpoints and thought processes in reaction to fresh knowledge or revelations. You become more open to a wider variety of options and solutions when you examine different interpretations of historical occurrences. This adaptability lessens cognitive rigidity and makes it easier to discard inflexible, counterproductive narratives.

Developing Gratitude and Appreciation: You are encouraged to develop gratitude and appreciation for the current moment by rewriting your story. You become more appreciative of life's rewards when you recognize how your prior experiences have molded your resilience and progress. Your attention is drawn to the wealth and beauty of the present rather than your old complaints when you concentrate on being grateful.

Accepting Adaptability and Resilience: Changing the way you tell your story encourages adaptability and resilience in the face of difficulty. You develop self-assurance and resourcefulness when you acknowledge your capacity to overcome obstacles and overcome setbacks. This resilience mentality strengthens the process of moving beyond previous traumas by enabling you to face challenges in the future with grace and resiliency.

Rephrasing your story can aid in the process of forgetting by separating you from the past, altering the emotional significance of memories, finding lessons and silver linings, strengthening your sense of self, encouraging cognitive flexibility, encouraging appreciation and thankfulness, and embracing resilience and adaptability. You may facilitate healing, development, and change by adopting a fresh viewpoint on the past, which enables you to go ahead with more inner peace, purpose, and clarity.

Cultivating a positive and empowering perspective on past experiences.

Cultivating a positive and empowering perspective on past experiences is a profound journey of self-discovery, healing, and personal growth. It requires courage, resilience, and a willingness to embrace the lessons embedded within our life's tapestry. Here are some key insights to help you cultivate such a perspective:

Embrace the Power of Perception: Recognize that your perspective shapes your reality. While you cannot change the past, you have the power to reinterpret your experiences through a lens of empowerment and growth. Shift your focus from dwelling on what went wrong to discerning the valuable lessons and insights gained from each experience.

Practice Gratitude for Lessons Learned: Cultivate a sense of gratitude for the wisdom gained from past experiences, even those that were challenging or painful. Every setback, disappointment, or hardship carries within it the seeds of growth and transformation. Embrace each experience as a teacher that has shaped you into the person you are today.

Reframe Challenges as Opportunities: Reframe challenges and setbacks as opportunities for growth and resilience. Rather than viewing obstacles as insurmountable barriers, see them as invitations to stretch beyond your comfort zone, develop new skills, and uncover hidden strengths. Embrace the journey of overcoming adversity with courage and determination.

Celebrate Your Resilience: Celebrate your resilience in the face of adversity. Reflect on the times when you have faced challenges head-on, navigated uncertainty with grace, and emerged stronger on the other side. Your ability to persevere in the face of difficulty is a testament to your inner strength and resilience.

Focus on What You Can Control: Focus your energy and attention on what you can control in the present moment rather than dwelling on the past or worrying about the future. Recognize that while you cannot change past events, you have the power to shape your present circumstances and create a fulfilling future.

Practice Self-Compassion: Be gentle and compassionate with yourself as you reflect on past experiences. Offer yourself the same kindness and understanding that you would extend to a dear friend facing similar challenges. Embrace your humanity—including your imperfections, vulnerabilities, and moments of struggle—with love and acceptance.

Set Intentions for Growth: Set intentions for growth and personal development based on the insights gained from past experiences. Identify areas of your life where you would like to cultivate greater resilience, compassion, authenticity, or fulfillment. Commit to taking intentional actions that align with your values and aspirations.

Seek Support and Connection: Seek support and connection from trusted friends, mentors, or counselors who can offer perspective, encouragement, and guidance as you navigate your journey of personal growth. Share your experiences openly and vulnerably with others, knowing that you are not alone on this path.

Cultivate a Mindset of Possibility: Cultivate a mindset of possibility and abundance, recognizing that each experience, whether positive or negative, holds within it the potential for growth and transformation. Approach life with curiosity, optimism, and a sense of adventure, embracing the unknown with courage and enthusiasm.

Live with Purpose and Intention: Live with purpose and intention, guided by a clear sense of values, passions, and aspirations. Align your actions with your deepest desires and aspirations, and commit to living a life that reflects your authentic self. Embrace each day as an opportunity to create meaning, connection, and joy.

By embracing a positive and empowering perspective on past experiences, you can transform challenges into opportunities, setbacks into stepping stones, and pain into wisdom. Embrace the journey of self-discovery and personal growth with an open heart and a willingness to learn from every twist and turn along the way.

Chapter 7: Self-Compassion and Self-Forgiveness

- The importance of forgiving oneself for harboring resentment.
- How self-compassion leads to a more forgiving and forgetful mindset.
- Practical exercises for self-forgiveness and letting go of self-blame.

The importance of forgiving oneself for harboring resentment.

A vital step in the forgiveness process is forgiving oneself for holding grudges, as it frees people from self-imposed shame, guilt, and self-blame and helps them on the path to recovery and inner peace. Here's why it's important to forgive oneself for holding grudges:

Self-acceptance and self-compassion: In order to forgive oneself for holding grudges, one must also embrace and show compassion for one's own humanity and flaws. It recognizes that everyone errs sometimes and feels wounded, angry, and resentful; these feelings are inherent to the human condition.

Releasing mental Burdens: Holding grudges against oneself may have a negative impact on one's mental health and cause emotions of shame, remorse, and self-blame. People who forgive themselves are able to experience more emotional freedom and resilience because they are released from the emotional weights that come with clinging onto previous transgressions or perceived failings.

Encouraging Personal Development and Healing: Allowing oneself to forgive for holding grudges makes room for personal development and healing. It helps people to consider the underlying causes of their resentment and to go above self-blame or self-criticism in order to learn from their experiences. Self-awareness, insight, and change are fostered by this process of introspection.

Breaking the Cycle of Self-Destructive Patterns: Holding grudges against oneself may encourage negative thinking and behavior patterns that feed self-destructive cycles of self-sabotage and negativity. People may break these habits and develop a better connection with themselves that is built on self-love, self-compassion, and self-respect by forgiving themselves.

Accepting Forgiveness as a Healing Practice: Self-forgiveness is the deliberate decision to let go of grudges from the past and welcome a future full of opportunities. It involves forgiving oneself for holding onto grudges. It acknowledges that forgiveness entails treating oneself with kindness and charity in addition to absolving others.

Restoring Self-Worth and Self-Esteem: Keeping grudges against oneself may damage one's self-worth and self-esteem, making it harder to feel confident and deserving of respect. People who forgive themselves embrace their intrinsic worth and dignity as human beings and acknowledge that they are worthy of love, compassion, and forgiveness from both themselves and other people.

Developing Inner Peace and Well-Being: Having inner peace and well-being is cultivated when one forgives themselves for holding grudges. It enables people to let go of the internal tensions and conflicts brought on by self-blame and self-judgment, which promotes more balance, harmony, and satisfaction in life.

To sum up, self-compassion, self-acceptance, and self-healing are transformed when one forgives oneself for holding onto grudges. It frees people from the chains of self-criticism and self-blame, paving the way for inner calm, resilience, and personal development. People may once again live really and fully, free from the weight of the past, when they accept forgiveness as a therapeutic practice.

How self-compassion leads to a more forgiving and forgetful mindset.

Self-compassion is essential for developing understanding, acceptance, and love toward oneself, which in turn helps one develop a more forgetting and forgiving perspective. Here's how self-compassion creates an attitude of amnesia and forgiveness:

Acknowledgment of Our Common Humanity: Self-compassion is acknowledging that imperfection and suffering are common experiences that all people share. When people compassionately accept their own shortcomings and hardships, they also accept that other people have similar difficulties. This acknowledgment of our shared humanity promotes empathy and comprehension, which facilitates forgiving oneself and other people.

Diminishment of Self-Criticism: Self-compassion is being nice and considerate to oneself in the same way that one would be to a friend in need. People may overcome self-criticism and self-judgment, which are often obstacles to forgetting and forgiving others, by practicing self-compassion. Rather of focusing on previous transgressions or self-perceived deficiencies, people treat themselves with compassion and empathy, making room for recovery and development.

Emotional Regulation: Self-compassion facilitates emotional regulation by enabling people to deal with challenging emotions more resolutely and easily. When anger, resentment, or pain arise, those who practice self-compassion are better able to calm themselves down with self-care and gentleness. This emotional control makes it easier for people to let go of grudges and lessens the intensity of unpleasant feelings, which promotes an attitude of amnesia and forgiving.

Release of ties to the previous: Self-compassion helps people let go of their ties to previous transgressions and complaints, which releases them from the weight of regret and bitterness. People may let go of strict expectations and perfectionistic impulses that hold them bound to the past by adopting a compassionate and accepting attitude toward oneself. People are able to go on more easily and openly when they let go of their attachments and embrace the present moment with a feeling of lightness and freedom.

Mindfulness Cultivation: Being mindful, or being aware of the current moment and accepting it without passing judgment, is strongly associated with self-compassion. People who practice self-compassion become more able to watch their thoughts and feelings with interest and transparency instead of responding to them hastily. By assisting people in letting go of excessive identification and rumination over the past, this attentive awareness promotes an attitude of amnesia and forgiveness.

Improvement of Self-Worth: By seeing people's innate worth and dignity, self-compassion improves one's own sense of self-worth and self-esteem. When people are nice and compassionate to themselves, they support a healthy self-image based on acceptance and dignity of oneself. Because they feel more valuable, people are able to forgive themselves for previous transgressions and let go of grudges, realizing that they deserve love and forgiveness.

In summary, self-compassion reduces self-criticism, promotes emotional control, releases ties to the past, cultivates awareness, and increases self-worth, all of which contribute to a more forgiving and forgetting perspective. People who use self-compassion as a compass may go ahead more easily and resiliently by fostering an atmosphere inside themselves that is forgiving, healing, and development.

Practical exercises for self-forgiveness and letting go of self-blame.

Compassion, self-awareness, and deliberate healing are all necessary on the transforming path of practicing self-forgiveness and letting go of self-blame. The following useful tasks will aid in this process:

Writing a Letter of Self-Forgiveness: Make time to compose a letter to yourself in which you ask for forgiveness for any perceived transgressions or shortfalls. Kindly and compassionately give yourself understanding and acknowledge whatever hurt or sorrow you may be hanging onto. Put more emphasis on self-compassion than self-blame. Writing on lessons learnt and affirmations of your own value is another option.

Self-Compassion Meditation: Focus on developing kindness toward yourself by doing a guided self-compassion meditation. Locate a peaceful area, shut your eyes, and recall an instance when you're experiencing self-blame issues. Say kind things to yourself, such as "May I forgive myself," "May I be kind to myself," and "May I let go of self-blame."

Self-reflection and mindfulness: Engage in mindfulness by objectively examining your feelings and thoughts. When self-blame creeps in, acknowledge it and gently bring your focus back to the here and now. To investigate the causes of self-blame and dispel any false or detrimental self-beliefs you may have, practice self-reflection.

Finding Patterns and Triggers: Keep an eye out for patterns or triggers that exacerbate feelings of guilt about oneself. Consider the circumstances, persons, or ways of thinking that often lead to self-criticism. You may create plans to deal with these triggers in a more considerate and productive way when they happen by recognizing them.

Affirmations and Positive Self-Talk: Develop self-compassion and combat self-blame by using affirmations and positive self-talk. Positive self-talk should be substituted with positive ones, such as "I am worthy of understanding and forgiveness," "I am human and imperfect, and that's okay," or "I choose to let go of self-blame and embrace self-compassion."

Self-Care Practices and Nurturing Activities: Take part in self-care and nurturing activities that help you feel better about yourself and restore your emotional reserves. This might be engaging in enjoyable hobbies, spending time in nature, getting adequate sleep, fueling your body with wholesome foods, and establishing supportive relationships with friends or family.

Seeking Assistance and Professional Assistance: Seek assistance and support from friends, family, or mental health experts to help you through the process of letting go of guilt and finding self-forgiveness. Openly and vulnerably discuss your experiences with people you trust, and if you need further help, think about going to therapy or counseling.

Realistic Expectations: Recognize your human limitations and try to create reasonable expectations for yourself. Recognize that making errors is a necessary component of learning and developing. Accept the idea that progress is more important than perfection and acknowledge your accomplishments along the way.

Recall that practicing self-forgiveness and letting go of guilt are continuous processes that call for perseverance, self-compassion, and dedication. As you travel this path, remember to treat yourself with kindness and have faith that you may develop more resilience, acceptance, and serenity inside yourself with practice and patience.

Chapter 8: Building Emotional Resilience

- **Strengthening emotional resilience to prevent relapses into resentment.**
- **Strategies for handling triggers and setbacks on the journey to forgetting.**
- **Cultivating a mindset that embraces growth and learning from past experiences.**

Strengthening emotional resilience to prevent relapses into resentment.

In order to avoid relapses into resentment and to promote an attitude of forgiveness, compassion, and inner peace, it is essential to strengthen emotional resilience. The following are useful techniques to improve emotional resilience:

Cultivate Self-Awareness: Gain a better comprehension of your feelings, stressors, and reaction patterns. Examine the root reasons of any bad feelings or resentment as soon as you see them. You may intervene early and put coping mechanisms in place before anger spirals out of control by developing your self-awareness.

Practice Mindfulness: Develop present-moment awareness and a nonjudgmental acceptance of your thoughts and feelings by practicing mindfulness. Being mindful enables you to see anger for what it is and avoid getting caught up in its narrative. Remaining rooted in the here and now allows you to react calmly and rationally to difficult circumstances.

Create a Supportive Network: Be in the company of mentors, family members, or friends who are encouraging, understanding, and empathic. Talk to trustworthy people about your challenges and experiences so they can provide you support and insight. Strong support systems increase resiliency and act as a buffer against the damaging impacts of anger.

Develop Coping Skills: Acquire and put into practice useful coping mechanisms to control stress, emotional swings, and resolve disputes with others in a positive way. Deep breathing exercises, aggressive communication, problem-solving tactics, and conflict resolution abilities are a few examples of these. Possessing a toolbox of coping mechanisms enables you to react to difficult circumstances in a flexible manner.

Set limits: To safeguard your mental health and stop anger from escalating in your relationships, set clear limits. Express your demands, principles, and boundaries in a courteous and forceful manner. Establishing boundaries promotes mutual respect and understanding between people as well as the maintenance of healthy dynamics.

Practice Forgiveness: Develop an attitude of forgiveness as a proactive strategy for settling disputes and getting rid of grudges. Realize that letting go of grudges and complaints releases you from the load of clinging onto them. Forgiveness is a gift that you offer yourself. As you continue to let go and move ahead with kindness and love, practice forgiveness.

Take Care of Yourself: Make frequent self-care activities that feed your mind, body, and soul a priority. This might include getting enough rest, working out often, maintaining a healthy diet, practicing relaxation methods, pursuing interests and hobbies, and looking for things that make you happy and fulfilled. Taking care of yourself makes you more resilient and better able to handle life's obstacles.

Promote Gratitude and Optimism: Even in the midst of hardship, have an optimistic mindset and concentrate on the good things in your life. By recognizing and appreciating the chances, gifts, and sustaining connections in your life, you may cultivate thankfulness. Gratitude and optimism building strengthens your resilience and keeps things in perspective when things are tough.

Seek Professional Support: You should think about getting help from a therapist, counselor, or mental health professional if your anger or other bad feelings start to become overpowering or persistent. Therapy may help you develop emotional resilience and stop resentful relapses by offering you insightful information, coping mechanisms, and support tailored to your own requirements.

By applying these techniques to your everyday life, you may develop an attitude of forgiveness, compassion, and inner peace as well as increase your emotional resilience. Developing emotional resilience gives you the tools you need to face life's obstacles head-on and come out on the other side with more satisfaction and well-being.

<u>**Strategies for handling triggers and setbacks on the journey to forgetting.**</u>

On the path to forgetting, managing triggers and obstacles calls for resiliency, self-awareness, and practical coping mechanisms. The following techniques can assist you in successfully navigating setbacks and triggers:

Determine Your Triggers: Invest some time in determining whether particular circumstances, ideas, or feelings lead to resentment or a return to unfavorable mental patterns. Knowing what sets you off enables you to prepare for difficult circumstances and use proactive coping mechanisms.

Practice Mindfulness: Develop awareness as a technique to watch triggers and obstacles without being overwhelmed by them. When triggers appear, take a minute to focus on the here and now. Without passing judgment, pay attention to your thoughts, feelings, and physical sensations and let them come and go as they may.

Apply Grounding strategies: Grounding strategies help you stay grounded in the here and now and lessen the impact of obstacles or triggers. When you feel overwhelmed, return to the present now by focusing on your breathing, using tactile things, or using your senses to notice your surroundings.

Develop Coping Skills: Get a toolkit of coping mechanisms and techniques to deal with stressors and disappointments in a productive way. This might be journaling, gradual muscle relaxation, deep breathing exercises, visualization methods, or doing things that make you happy and comfortable.

Challenge Negative Thoughts: Use cognitive restructuring strategies to confront negative ideas and attitudes that surface in reaction to obstacles or triggers. Examine the truth of your ideas and take into account more realistic and balanced viewpoints. Affirmations and kind self-statements should take the place of negative self-talk.

Ask for Help: When faced with triggers or setbacks, don't be afraid to ask for help and direction from friends, family, or mental health specialists. Talk honestly and vulnerably about your experiences with people you can trust to provide perspective, understanding, and affirmation.

Have Reasonable Expectations: Acknowledge that obstacles are a normal part of the process of moving beyond the past and forgiving others. When things become hard, remember to treat yourself with love and compassion and set reasonable expectations for yourself. Accept failures as chances for development, education, and perseverance.

Practice Self-Compassion: On your road to forgetting, manage triggers and obstacles with kindness and compassion for yourself. Give yourself the same consideration and compassion that you would provide to a friend going through a comparable situation. To cultivate your inner resilience and wellbeing, try self-soothing methods and affirmations.

Learn from Setbacks: See setbacks as instructive events that reveal your triggers, weak points, and places in which you may improve. Think back on the things you've learnt from failures and how you can use them to improve your coping mechanisms and resilience in the future.

Remain Committed to recovery: In spite of obstacles or setbacks, remain dedicated to your recovery process. Keep in mind that recovery is a gradual process and that obstacles are only meant to be temporary diversionary routes. As you go on your journey of forgetting and forgiving yourself, remember to be kind, persistent, and gentle with yourself.

You may successfully manage obstacles and triggers on your path to forgetting by putting these tactics into practice, which will also help you develop more resilience, self-awareness, and inner peace along the road.

Cultivating a mindset that embraces growth and learning from past experiences.

The development of a growth-oriented and experience-learning mentality is crucial for resilience, emotional health, and personal progress. The following techniques can assist you in cultivating this mindset:

Practice Self-Reflection: Make time for introspection and self-reflection to examine your prior choices, obstacles, and experiences. Think back on the lessons you have gained from these encounters and the ways in which they have aided in your own development.

Embrace a Growth Mindset: Develop a growth mindset by thinking that your skills, knowledge, and aptitudes can be enhanced with commitment, hard work, and persistence. Accept problems as chances for personal development rather than as something to avoid. Have faith in your own abilities, and in your ability to grow and learn.

Honor Progress Rather Than Perfection: Prioritize progress over perfection by acknowledging and appreciating your little triumphs and accomplishments along the way. Understand that progress is a slow process with obstacles and setbacks. Appreciate your perseverance and hard work regardless of the result.

Learn from Mistakes and Setbacks: Consider errors and setbacks as priceless chances for development. Rather of obsessing on mistakes or disappointments, recognize the lessons they provide and think about how you might use them in your next attempts. As you traverse the highs and lows of life, adopt an attitude of inquiry and discovery.

Seek Support and Feedback: Remain receptive to other people's opinions, whether they are encouraging or constructive criticism. As you work to learn and develop, surround yourself with encouraging friends, mentors, or coworkers who can provide direction, a different viewpoint, and support.

Establish Meaningful Objectives: Establish attainable objectives that are consistent with your beliefs, passions, and dreams. Deconstruct more ambitious objectives into more doable, smaller stages, and acknowledge your accomplishments as you go. Remain adaptable and modify your objectives in light of fresh information and experiences.

Build Resilience: Build resilience via the acquisition of coping mechanisms, methods for controlling emotions, and a solid support system. Having resilience makes it easier and more flexible for you to overcome hardships, obstacles, and failures. Accept setbacks as chances to fortify your inner resources and develop resilience.

Practice Gratitude: Develop an attitude of thankfulness by taking time each day to consider the advantages, opportunities, and fulfilling experiences you have had in your life. Give thanks for the lessons you've learnt from the past, especially the tough and painful ones. Having gratitude improves resilience in the face of hardship and cultivates an optimistic attitude.

Remain Curious and Open to New Experiences: Remain open-minded and receptive to new ideas, viewpoints, and chances for personal development. Go outside your comfort zone and meet the unknown with an open mind and a spirit of adventure. Be open to absorbing knowledge from a variety of sources.

Emphasis on the Journey: Accept the path of personal development and exploration instead of being obsessed with the end point. Appreciate the learning, discovery, and self-improvement process just as much as—if not more than—the outcome. Accept change and uncertainty as necessary components on the path to personal development and fulfillment.

You give yourself the ability to face life's obstacles with resiliency, curiosity, and optimism when you accept progress and learn from the past. Accept every event as a chance for personal development and self-awareness, and relish the process of evolving into your greatest self.

Chapter 9: Embracing Inner Peace and Moving Forward

- The culmination of the forgiveness and forgetting process.
- Embracing the inner peace that comes with letting go.
- Practical tips for moving forward, building a fulfilling future, and maintaining a mindset of forgiveness.

The culmination of the forgiveness and forgetting process.

The culmination of the forgiveness and forgetting process is marked by a profound sense of inner peace, freedom, and emotional liberation. It represents a transformative journey of healing, growth, and self-discovery that enables individuals to release the burdens of resentment, pain, and attachment to the past. Here are some key elements of the culmination of the forgiveness and forgetting process:

Emotional Liberation: At the culmination of the forgiveness and forgetting process, individuals experience a profound sense of emotional liberation and release. They no longer feel burdened by the weight of past grievances, resentments, or grudges. Instead, they experience a lightness of being and a newfound sense of emotional freedom.

Inner Peace: Forgiveness and forgetting pave the way for inner peace—a deep sense of tranquility and harmony that emanates from within. Individuals no longer feel consumed by anger, bitterness, or regret. Instead, they cultivate a sense of serenity and acceptance that transcends external circumstances.

Letting Go of Attachments: The culmination of the forgiveness and forgetting process involves letting go of attachments to the past—whether it be painful memories, resentments toward others, or self-blame and guilt. Individuals release the grip of past experiences and embrace the present moment with openness and clarity.

Renewed Relationships: Forgiveness often paves the way for renewed or transformed relationships with others. Individuals who have gone through the forgiveness process may experience deeper connections, greater empathy, and improved communication with those they have forgiven. Relationships are infused with a sense of authenticity and compassion.

Self-Compassion and Self-Acceptance: At the culmination of the forgiveness and forgetting process, individuals cultivate a profound sense of self-compassion and self-acceptance. They learn to treat themselves with kindness, understanding, and forgiveness, recognizing their inherent worthiness and dignity as human beings.

Living in the Present Moment: Forgiveness and forgetting enable individuals to embrace the present moment fully. They no longer dwell on past grievances or anxieties about the future. Instead, they immerse themselves in the richness and beauty of each moment, savoring the experiences and connections that life has to offer.

Personal Growth and Transformation: The culmination of the forgiveness and forgetting process represents a journey of personal growth and transformation. Individuals emerge from the process with a deeper understanding of themselves, greater resilience in the face of adversity, and an expanded capacity for love, empathy, and compassion.

Integration of Lessons Learned: Throughout the forgiveness and forgetting process, individuals integrate the lessons learned from their experiences into their lives. They recognize the wisdom gained from past challenges and apply it to navigate future obstacles with grace and wisdom.

In summary, the culmination of the forgiveness and forgetting process is a profound and transformative journey toward inner peace, emotional liberation, and personal growth. It involves letting go of past grievances, embracing the present moment with openness and acceptance, and cultivating deeper connections with oneself and others. Through forgiveness and forgetting, individuals unlock the door to a life filled with love, compassion, and authenticity.

Embracing the inner peace that comes with letting go.

It takes bravery, self-awareness, and a willingness to give up control to life's course to embrace the inner serenity that comes with letting go. The following are essential actions to accept the inner tranquility that comes with letting go:

Acceptance of What Is: To start, acknowledge and embrace the truth of the current situation, along with whatever feelings, situations, or connections you may be clinging to. Acceptance is the ability to accept things as they are without struggle or condemnation, not a passive surrender.

Release Attachment to Results: Part of letting go is freeing oneself from expectations or certain results. Realize that there are things in life beyond your control and that clinging to strict expectations will only make you feel frustrated and disappointed. Adopt an open-minded, adaptable mentality and let life develop naturally.

Give Up Worries About the Past and Future and Practice Surrendering to the Present: Let Go of Your Worries About the Past and Future. Concentrate on the present moment and truly savor its beauty by bringing all of your attention to it. Practice being present and aware of everything that you do.

Kindness and Forgiveness: As you let go, show kindness and forgiveness to both yourself and other people. Let go of any self-blame, grudges, or lingering resentment that could be holding you down. Adopt a forgiving mentality as a means of achieving emotional freedom and healing.

Have faith in the universe: Develop faith in the universe's innate wisdom and order. Have faith that everything occurs for a purpose, even if we don't always understand it at the time, and that life has a way of working itself out in its own time. Have faith in your ability to bounce back from setbacks and handle life's obstacles with dignity and grace.

Practice Non-Attachment: Part of letting go is learning to be detached from things that define you, including identities, roles, and material belongings. Realize that your inner nature transcends circumstances and that, whatever accomplishments or external affirmation, you are entire and complete in your core.

Accept Impermanence: Acknowledge that everything in life is temporary and that impermanence is a fact. Recognize that stability and security are temporary, and that clinging to them will only cause you pain. Accept impermanence as a liberating force and give yourself permission to go with life's ever-changing currents.

Develop a Gratitude Attitude: Develop an attitude of thankfulness for all of life's opportunities, lessons, and benefits. Make it a habit to be grateful every day, seeing the beauty and plenty all around you. Gratitude creates a profound feeling of inner serenity and satisfaction and opens your heart to the present.

Seek Meaning and Purpose: Consider the more profound significance and reason for your goals and experiences. Make a connection with your deepest aspirations, beliefs, and interests to ensure that your actions reflect your true priorities. Instead than focusing just on your exterior accomplishments or milestones, find joy in the trip itself.

Develop Self-Compassion: When you go through the process of letting go, treat yourself with kindness and compassion. Be kind, compassionate, and patient with yourself, particularly when you're struggling or unsure about anything. Develop an affectionate connection with oneself that is founded on self-love and self-care.

Accepting the inner serenity that accompanies relinquishing control allows you to step into a life of more autonomy, happiness, and satisfaction. Letting go is about believing in your own heart's wisdom and submitting to life's natural flow, not about giving up or losing control. Discover the deep serenity that is waiting for you on the other side when you embrace the process of letting go with bravery, openness, and grace.

Practical tips for moving forward, building a fulfilling future, and maintaining a mindset of forgiveness.

Making deliberate efforts, reflecting on oneself, and committing to one's own development are necessary for moving ahead, creating a meaningful future, and keeping an attitude of forgiving. The following useful advice can assist you in navigating this journey:

Establish Specific Goals and Intentions: Based on your beliefs, interests, and ambitions, establish specific goals and intentions for your future. Make a strategy to accomplish your objectives by breaking them down into manageable chunks. You may go ahead with purpose and intention when you have a clear idea of where you are going.

Keep Your Eyes on the Present: Setting objectives for the future is great, but don't lose sight of the here and now. Make the most of every minute by concentrating on what you can accomplish right now to get closer to your objectives. Being attentive may help you maintain your composure and attention in the here and now.

Develop Self-Compassion: As you go through life's ups and downs, treat yourself with kindness and compassion. Show yourself the same compassion and consideration that you would provide to a friend going through a comparable situation. While you strive for your objectives, prioritize your well-being and engage in self-care.

Practice Gratitude: Develop a grateful mindset by consistently recognizing and appreciating the chances and gifts in your life. Spend some time thinking about all the things, no matter how little, for which you are grateful. Having gratitude makes you feel good and keeps things in perspective when things are tough.

Embrace Resilience: Develop resilience by seeing obstacles and failures as chances for development and education. Consider challenges as stepping stones toward your objectives rather than as barriers. Adopt a resilient mentality that will allow you to overcome hardship and emerge stronger than before.

Forgive Others and Yourself: Let go of grudges and move on with clarity and serenity of mind by forgiving yourself and others. Forgive others for whatever hurt they may have caused you, and forgive yourself for your previous transgressions and failings. Recall that you are giving yourself a gift when you forgive.

Solution: When confronted with obstacles, concentrate on identifying solutions rather than lingering on the issue. Become proactive in your thinking so that you may overcome hurdles and take action. Divide issues into doable stages and ask for help when you need it.

Seek Support and Connection: When you need help and connection, don't be scared to ask for it. Be in the company of upbeat, encouraging individuals who see the potential in you and motivate you to achieve your goals. Create a support system of classmates, friends, and mentors who encourage and motivate you.

Celebrate Your Achievements: Don't forget to give yourself a pat on the back for all of your accomplishments. No matter how little, acknowledge your victories and growth. Honoring your accomplishments gives you more self-assurance and drive to keep going.

Keep Your Mind Open to Change and development: Accept change and development as normal parts of life. Remain receptive to fresh viewpoints, experiences, and possibilities that present themselves. Stay open to changing and growing as you go on your path to a happy and meaningful future.

You may go on with confidence, create a meaningful future, and maintain an attitude of forgiveness that promotes serenity, resiliency, and personal development by implementing these useful suggestions into your day-to-day activities. Keep in mind that you are on a continuous path towards living a life filled with meaning and satisfaction with every step you take.

Conclusion: The Freedom of Forgetting

- **Reflecting on the transformative journey from resentment to forgetting.**
- **Encouragement to continue practicing forgiveness and forgetting for a life filled with inner peace and resilience.**

Reflecting on the transformative journey from resentment to forgetting.

There is a great chance to recognize the development, healing, and inner change that have taken place along the road as one looks back on the transforming path from resentment to forgetfulness. Some important thoughts about this trip are as follows:

Acknowledgment of Resentment: Consider the original resentment that may have had a negative impact on your heart and thoughts. Recognize whatever sadness, grief, and rage you may have had as a consequence of injustices or grievances from the past.

Courage to Confront Emotions: Consider the bravery required to face and investigate your feelings, even when they are upsetting or unpleasant. Acknowledge your own resilience and strength to address your emotions head-on with kindness and honesty.

Recognizing the Sources of Resentment: Consider the underlying reasons and situations that have caused your resentment. Think back to the experiences, ideas, and incidents that helped animosity accumulate over time. Examine the thinking and behavior patterns that keep you mired in a resentment and rage cycle.

Decision to Forgive: Consider the crucial instance in which you chose to forgive consciously. Think about what made you decide to let go of the past and follow a road of forgiveness and healing. Acknowledge the agency and power that come with using forgiveness as a transforming practice.

Accepting the forgiving Process: Consider the forgiving process itself, including the breakthrough and enlightening moments as well as the doubtful and resistant ones. Honor all of your accomplishments and landmarks along the route, no matter how little. Accept forgiveness as a process that happens gradually rather than all at once.

Developing Self-Compassion: Consider how crucial it is to take care of yourself and your path at all times. Acknowledge the importance of being kind, forgiving, and understanding with yourself, particularly when you're feeling vulnerable or doubting yourself. Accept self-compassion as your compass for moving toward recovery.

Letting Go of Resentment: Consider how you might gradually let go of resentment and free your heart and mind from its hold. As you release the grip of old grudges and give yourself permission to consider new options, pay attention to the times when you give in and embrace yourself. Honor the freedom that comes from letting go.

Accepting the Forgetfulness Aspect: Contemplate the importance of accepting forgetfulness as a necessary step on the path to inner tranquility and recovery. Understand that forgetting does not imply eliminating the past; rather, it is relinquishing its authority to shape your present and future. Accept forgetting as a gift of emancipation and rejuvenation.

Embracing Growth and Transformation: Consider the development, change, and inner knowledge that have resulted from the passage from bitterness to forgetting. Appreciate the resilient, kind, and forgiving person you have grown into. Respect the knowledge and fortitude acquired throughout the journey.

Commitment to Ongoing Development: Consider your dedication to ongoing development, recovery, and self-discovery. Accept the trip as a continuous process of renewal and development that offers chances for growth, connection, and satisfaction. Make a commitment to fostering an attitude of compassion, forgiveness, and inner serenity in every aspect of your life.

Pay tribute to the breadth of your experiences and the bravery required to set out on this road of recovery and rejuvenation as you consider the transforming journey from resentment to forgetfulness. Accept the trip with an open heart, appreciation, and compassion, understanding that every step you take will bring you one step closer to living a complete and genuine life.

Encouragement to continue practicing forgiveness and forgetting for a life filled with inner peace and resilience.

Dear friend,

As you journey through the path of forgiveness and forgetting, I want to offer you words of encouragement and support. This journey you have embarked upon is one of profound transformation—one that leads to inner peace, resilience, and freedom from the burdens of the past.

Know that every step you take toward forgiveness and forgetting is a courageous act of self-love and healing. It takes strength to confront the pain and resentment that may have lingered within your heart for so long. But by choosing forgiveness, you are choosing liberation—you are choosing to reclaim your power and rewrite your story.

In moments of doubt or struggle, remember the profound impact that forgiveness can have on your life. It is not merely about letting go of past grievances, but about reclaiming your present and future. It is about releasing the chains of resentment that have bound you and embracing the boundless possibilities that await you.

Forgiveness is a gift you give to yourself—a gift of inner peace, resilience, and empowerment. It is a testament to your strength and capacity for growth. And as you continue to practice forgiveness, know that you are paving the way for a life filled with authenticity, connection, and joy.

But forgiveness is not always easy, and there may be moments when the journey feels overwhelming. During those times, lean on the support of loved ones, mentors, and your own inner wisdom. Allow yourself grace and compassion as you navigate the complexities of healing.

Remember, too, that forgetting is not about erasing the past, but about releasing its hold over your present. It is about choosing to live fully in the present moment, unencumbered by the weight of old wounds. It is about embracing the beauty and possibility of each new day with a heart that is open and free.

As you continue to walk this path, may you find strength in the knowledge that you are not alone. Countless others have traveled this journey before you, and countless others will follow in your footsteps. Together, we are united in our quest for healing, wholeness, and peace.

So keep moving forward, one step at a time, knowing that each moment of forgiveness brings you closer to the life you deserve—a life filled with love, joy, and resilience. Embrace the journey with courage, knowing that the destination is worth every moment of struggle and every tear shed along the way.

With love and encouragement,

Kendra T. Keeton

Other Books By Kendra T. Keeton

Healing From Abuse

How To Deal With Toxic People

How To Find Inner Peace

How To Heal From Infidelity

How To Raise Good Humans